salt + honey

secular prayers to the human and hedonistic hearts

Isabel Abbott

ISBN: 978-0-692-72343-2

dedication:

for jamal
for dr. Julie
for you

To the human animals; to the long lost and the finally found—to the freedom in taking your own life into your arms and loving hard.

This is for you, for me, for all of us.
The ones who seek and say the names for the unspoken and outcast, who linger with intimacy at the glory of the secular world, who no longer wait for removal of old injuries and instead wear scars with defiance and the softest love. The ones who reinvent the old myths and reclaim the unbound slips of skin that lived between and beneath the words,
who do not clamor for the world beyond but choose this,

here,

fallen in love with the breath that lives
close to the bone.

Whether you believe or do not believe, in the gods or the body's language unbended or the arrows that point in forever opposing directions, what I know is this:
We are all deserving of the words of devotion.
So this is for all of us here, in the living. I wrote us words like driftwood thrown from sea to shore, collecting them together with heart valves like rope to tie strong, giving language to the Salt and Honey of secular psalms and unholy hymns, a lexicon for the humans with our clutched fists and waking want, our adaptation and resistance, our dark and diaphanous light.

Yours in love and life before death,
Isabel

Contents

Prayer

[prair]

noun

1. a devout offering to the secular earth or object of adoration.
2. connection to divinity without the divine, as in gratitude, unspoken secrets, honoring for the irreverent.
3. love letters, sometimes.
4. an earnest wish and the held breath of hope.
5. me, speaking to you.

muse

Red rover red rover, send shattering light on over.
Send love over.
Send your cracked sidewalk heart and blistered corridors over.
Send everything you promised but could not keep over.
Send the wayward and the want over
and come crashing through

I would do everything, all of it, all over again

The way, when driving through the hills of Tennessee, the leaves were in a riot, like redemption is marching red. And how we passed an old dilapidated carnival, the rides and signs rusting and peeling paint, faded and frightening, echoes of old melancholy. And how I remembered, then, the how.

How I love abandoned places. How they speak of
impermanence and what remains,
memories kept in the pockets of torn jeans.
How the sight of this city's skyline lit up at night, when
returning and seeing it at a distance and then in the
knot of her streets, will never cease to be beautiful to me.
The importance of good silk, lingering against skin. The taste of
the ocean.
How a person can become home.

root

Radical. Revolution.
Starting with learning to love differently.
Starting with me.

benediction

for firsts.
lasts.
bruised shoulders
and prodigal needs.
smooth of cherry and sea glass, soft of parted lip.
life, you are so reckless. bitter bite.
relentless and bright as orange trees.
devout like monastic call to prayer, hungry as new love.

dear night (hallowed)

you are my kind of beauty.

love,
the dark light

hearts and bone

If scars are stories
(the kind we cling to so as to not tip into the fault line of fading memory, or else woefully leave us wanting in their anticlimactic irrelevance).
If scars are the body on parade,
wounds of war and emblems of achievement.
If scars are secrets of what we don't speak,
and dull ache of things split
and taken
and the most honest exhibition of what healing really is with its closed over skin and forever raised welt.

If this is a scar, then bones are beyond and beneath, the hidden and that which holds together,
the strange shapes we make of our lives and loving,
our repetitions and compulsions, our insistence and swelter
and slit cavern that houses a heart.
Bones are the dust and mineral and hard sharp and surprising soft that even the scars can't see.

So here I stand, feeling their clanging hurt, listening for their indecipherable language:
navigation of north and equator and crossroad
ancient, Cain, clear as a night sky in cold winter
unbearable light
indescribable wonder
heresy and home, every time you opened a door and every time you kept contained, the word that you can
never quite find, the one about how even memory can change.

rich with loss

Laying things down,
hands open like the unfurled fronds of palm trees.
Open enough to receive. To release. To breathe again easy,
even in the great grief.
Even, especially, in the grief.

petrichor

There are moments[1] when something in me, in life,
in the story we never understand but are always
trying to tell,
knows a kind of completeness.

---

[1] (this was one of those)

salt + honey

To Frida

If I pray, it is to her. Her willingness to make art from the broken and believing body, the hybridity of identity and voice, the wandering womb, the love that decides when and where it will be spilled out, without apology.

Do you think if we could go back we would tell ourselves what happens?[2]

If we could go back, to go visit who we were then, trying on our new identities as mothers, the room where we first met, and then discarding the new mom's group to go begin writing again, insistent that we keep our artist selves alive. If we could go back, to where we brought our babies and drank coffee and realized we did recall how to do the Heimlich maneuver and how we didn't know then all that would happen. If we could go back, would we tell ourselves everything that was going to happen?

"I would tell us this," I said. "Not everything. But this." That eleven years later, we would be changed, and we would still be here, after all this time, together. I would tell us that this would become its own true love. And we all need it, need this, the one who was there then and who is here now, helping you hang your shower curtain and mixing martinis and saying this is where you get your whole self back again, all your life belonging to you.

---

[2] the question asked when helping a friend of eleven years move out of her house and into her life, five years after she had done the same for me.

salt + honey

held on hard floor

Slipping into night
stretch out, now,
listen.

(i want. i want. i want.)

I want to be where the bats fly free, slow and half way hidden,
The wild mass of them storming the bridge, the thumping
breath of them in the cave of clear water, the ache of them,
dark and diaphanous.
I want an abundance of splayed flowers, all white,
and the missing to be met.
To know the word for lucky in every language.
Liquid with so much salt I enter altered states, and an
understanding of ancestors.
Dirt. The unimagined
I want to meet in the space between what we mean when we
say god
and what we know when love disrupts.

adaptation

In the world of big words and a sore body and a mind
quickening
with the love for learning,
the refuge of the bed we will tumble into at the end of days of
separate and together,
music I used to striptease to comes on over the radio where I
sit now writing,
the ice nearly melted in the thick glass and the humidity still
clinging to skin.
This. Perfect in a way I cannot yet unfasten but know as the life
I want. This. What I have chosen.

For all the hurt lines and hearts beating strong.
For all the change and the things that can never be undone,
and the windows that glow in the night.
For all the inevitable regrets, the mystery to which I offer all of
me, and the move toward freedom for all people.
For all the dreams of linen sheets and the taste you spit, the
words you slipped, into my mouth; undoing me.
My answer is yes.

"Except," you said, "I don't pray"

It is late.
You do not know what prayer is right now, in this
moment. No, not ever really, and not now,
when you are numb and dumb and disbelieving.
And you don't understand life, its silky skin and all the
broken things, how when you woke in the night you
settled into the comfort of her breathing,
burrowing into the soft cotton of her shirt,
and for this you felt both guilty and grateful.

But dear god, the lights were beautiful.
It was your first night flying lesson, wings hovering and
suspended in the dark,
the hum more like a hush.
How quiet inside it feels, focused and clear and like
nothingness that is somehow the center of everything
you do not know. The dark. And the lights scattered.
The illumination of life below, how you wanted to cry
cracks through the streets and you knew nothing of
prayer or life. But the lights were beautiful, and so too
the movement that was stillness. And you don't know
why you get to be here, alive, pulsing. But you are.
You are here, you are here, you are here.

you. finding me.

quiet and soft as moths,
stubborn as locked knees,
suggestive as the image on the inside of eyelids,
right before tumbling to sleep.

(un)holy prayer to Saturday

For the black slip with the strap that slips off shoulder.
For a return to the fist and the floor, and the way the
body remembers. For storm warnings and crashing trees
and water telling the story my mouth cannot yet find.
For burial sites where I remember and the one I still
reach for. For locating language
in the rush of speed and soft skin of thigh.
For hands cutting flight from printed pages.
Thank you, for your refuge and your terrible scars and
your joy.

wandering womb

Myth. Old, old stories. The ones about why women were created, what they are good for, what they need, what they should never be allowed. The ones about function, about rightful place, about the mystery, about shelter. There are these moments, when I am lying still outside, in grass or sand or carried on water, and I think I can feel them, the cells of them,
all the thousands of years of stories about the hollow inside me,
which once housed a uterus, which is still the source from which
I listen and speak. The old stories - I no longer carry the weight of them, and so these days I walk lighter on this earth. But I'd be lying if I said they were not woven into everything, and to hear my womb words is to first give voice to everything told in its origins. The way you bleed a thing out, give it back to its rightful owner, and in the quiet that then comes, you hear, finally,
a voice to call your own.

Vigil

For all those in the dark and the dying.
May you be honored.
May your name be held holy.
May your body know comfort.
May a flicker of this love somehow find you,
and may you know yourself as held, here, in the light.

lineage

For every woman, every artist, who dared to live
and love and create beyond the categories given
and the rooms offered,
who chose instead to invent the world inside out,
thank you.
Somehow you reach through all times,
and it is less lonely, more possible,
to own my own life as belonging to me.

You who had no children are my mothers.

salt + honey

come here to me

comfort, in being and becoming.
deep dark and soft white.
silk cotton and thread count.
folded corners and unkempt love.

to you, right next to me and you all those miles away

Thank you, for everything you did to survive, to live, to arrive to this now, this here, this early May day where in my own city it is like we've been baptized in summer and everyone is running around in torn shorts, digging hands into dirt and shaking off the last of the thaw by the lake. Thank you. Thank you for scraping through and sweeping sleep from a too tired face and feeling half frozen, half hyper-alert while you sat there at the laundromat plotting your next book. Thank you for making the decisions that everyone saw and how some loved you and some hated you and you stood there solid, and for the decisions no one could see but you and how these were the ones that made it hard to rest and that set you free. Thank you for making things, mending things, following the river. Thank you for asking questions and stomping truth and falling in love again even after all those years, and you thought that kind of thing had left you a long time ago but there you were, falling and falling and falling. Thank you for not giving up and thank you for your collapse and knowing to say no more. Thank you for grieving, for letting the loss come and change all the shapes so your very body had to rearrange its form, and how you didn't think you would survive and now you know some part of you did not, but you are here, missing and whole. Thank you for the night when you were eighteen and rode in the back up the pick-up truck and understood the meaning of the star's silence. For not knowing your own name, and for burning the bridge, and for breaking the law.

For swearing you'd start over and waking up the next day only to recognize you were in the cycle that was not yet ready to close, and so the covers come up and the substance is consumed and you find the way through the fog. Thank you for starting over.

For the cuts in your legs, and the birth, and the change in plans. For the walking away and the banging down doors and the evolution so slow you didn't know it was happening until you looked backwards and saw the trail you left like clothes discarded one by one on the way to the bed. Thank you. I know it wasn't easy. I know it almost killed you.

Survival is breathtaking and breathgiving. But it is not free. It is terribly expensive. And of great value. And you chose it. And today it is warm and lilacs take over the sidewalk and I'm sitting here in mad respect and true love for the life that keeps wanting to happen. And for you.

sister winter

sometimes it happens that way, the beauty of thing
breaking through,
a living myth,
stars of paper and white petals.

I was within and without

There is a kind of hushed happiness in returning and seeing
from below the neon glow of blue
filling the room and world above.
It is almost like prayer
or what we have after the words I love you
or what will reside when you let go everything you once told
yourself about who you were or would become.

invitation

Bring your skinned knees and tree sap tangled hair.
Bring your memories you can never make sense of and the
restless movement toward life
everything allowed, everything broken, everything bare and
luxurious and revealed,
the grief that slams all the cupboards
but they never stay shut,
the love that says come home to me.

Bring the creek that walks wide into unknowns, and the caves
where the dark wings of light live, and the stillness when you
knew in that moment you were real.
Bring your stunned clutch, and your fear, and your rage only he
will ever understand.
Bring your need for a closing and your bruised arms and your
uncombed hair, your slashed scar and your
tongue still stained.

Bring your need, your mouth that loves black licorice and your
jagged stitched mending.
Bring the fields of desert flowers.
Bring your monsoon and your doubts, your intact bones and
your rain soaked kissing,
opening the back door every morning,
everything you ever
tried to leave behind, living now in your skin.

No matter how many times you have left.
No matter how many times you have wondered at the waking.
No matter the injuries or the unwanted or the pleasure that
felt indecent in its honest asking.

Even when you broke your vow.
Even when you turned against yourself.
Even when you tried everything you had but you could not
save them, take them with you.
Even when you still stood there,
pulsing and alive, Lazarus.
Even. No matter. Because of this.
You are welcome here.

So bring what wrecks you and what sustains you,
what haunts you and heals you.
Come, again and again.
I will stay with you.

Hungry

(like craving. like you could devour the whole world. like you would say no to everything and keep the longing loose in your mouth until only that which truly satisfies comes and meets you here where you are. like missing. like love.)

Hungry

for gatherings of things. A table filled with flowers, too many to count. A sky filled with birds in migration, crying awe. A fist filled with memory, hiding marked lines,
rushing of water from sky to turbulent ocean.
For heat.
For poetry, and hair pulled, and names spoken.

For blank space. Empty walls. White rooms. Open roads.
The unmarked page, waiting. those slender slips of time when
it is like something stops, or suspends in air,
and you will never be able to say what happened,
how magnificent the quiet was, but it was enough that
you were there. For those breaths of seconds,
your eyes were opened.

For meaning.
Not found, but made.
Not ordained, but chosen.
Not arrived at, but birthed from the mess of love and the
body that protests and knows pleasure and the breath that
animates and orients toward light.

beginning

"I'm scared," I said.
"What if it all ends? Or just falls apart? What if I'm left with all the ashes and broken things again?"

"You know," she said.
"You don't have to decide the ending
before it's even started."

beginning again

Let's tell the truth today; the truth that lives in our bodies and
our nightscape dreams and our cells which are forever
connecting and coming undone. Let's know where we stand,
and stand there strong and with all the love we have ever
received and offered. Even if it didn't turn out the way
we thought it would or wanted. Even if it was not forever.
Even if we never knew their name.
It was love, and will be the ground if we let it.

Let's turn ourselves upside down, confusions of wonder, and
how it feels when you lie on the table and let your head drift
off the side, your hair a tumble reaching toward floor. Let's
care enough to really care, to show up and offer from the well
of our own wounding and restoration, and let's learn how to
care this deeply and still laugh this hard, not taking ourselves
so seriously we forget that none of us really knows what we
are doing and we can show up and love true anyways. Let's
make messes - on the wall and on the page and in the bed and
out in the world where we just might find our true home if we
walked up and spoke to a stranger. Let's make up all our own
rules and then break them. Let's order room service in a hotel
room with white sheets and whispered words. Let's leave
flowers in places where there has been cruelty. Let's paint
maps on our bodies and write wisdom on our skin.

Today is as good a day as any, to love what we love,
and be as we truly are, and decide
we are done waiting for our real lives to begin.

this body is your home

be a soft landing for yourself.

unbound

The throat wants to open.
The sound wants to be spoken.
The voice wants to be heard
in the body and ballot,
the birth room and the blank page,
the art and the protest,
the glittering and rusted truths.

rouse

after a long winter, bare legs are so beautiful.[3]
skin to air, returned to myself,
the first flutter of freedom.

[3] walking on the tops of tall buildings.

Breaking ground

1. I feel what cannot be named about the inescapable
   ecstasy and chaos of living in a body. How it has been
   a battlefield, the site source of another's violence.
   How it has been desperate to be fed and
   found wanting of what it needed.
   How it is the truth, the way, and the life.
   How it lets me settle deep into a home of belonging
   with the simple act and ease and stretching from the
   waist and wrapping my arms around legs. How it
   knows what feels good. How it is where the house of
   grief lives, and where the love knows its welcoming,
   and where the war is waged.

2. There is no such thing as a holy war.

when pressed up against the unknowns

What is clear is that some things need no explanation,
as if their very existence is the answered asking
or the inevitable outcome of the myths or
re-remembered undone legend.
Like the pink of peonies, the strength of horses, the bruised
and bleeding palm, the breaking of clocks.

What is clear is that I will follow you into the dark,
hold vigil in the night,
light the candles and guard the gate.

What is clear is that when the warm comes,
when the windows open and the fog lifts and the
heat starts early in the morning even before coffee has cooled.
When the reminder of my limbs loosened becomes the
language of knowing again my true origins.
When the warm comes, I come home.

What is clear is the shape her mouth makes in rapt attention
the conviction of love
the pause that happens when the birds are
sitting on the stretched wire, right before they take flight.

dear life

you are so vicious, and so beautiful.
i can't help it, the falling in love with you,
each time its own shocked and still wonder.

what seems important, upon first meeting you

fragile but bullet proof
(which is what my ribs once told her)
a heart made of thick jungle, and flickering neon signs,
and a bathtub filled with black sunshine.[4]

---

[4] naming

devotion

There is no sense to be made,
because I have given
more than my pound of flesh,
and yet the terms of engagement for living never suggested
any of this was or ever would be fair or reasonable,
would be anything other than this inexplicable random
colliding of cells and stars.

But I'm still here, and I belong here, to this,
the world.

I love her.

So I bring my carved into body and my clawed devotion,
and I lay it out like offerings.
I chose to be here; she chose to have me,
this is all that is known in the end.

reckoning

Liquid sky and velvet water.
I come to leave things.
I find myself.

testify

Because the beating sound the heart makes is the clap of valve cusps opening and closing. Which means, to stay alive we must open and close and open. Again and again and again. Because the match was lit by your own hand, and the house burned to the ground, and you thought maybe there was no corner left to turn, revealing unexpected doors, gifts. Only here you are, the smoke still stained to your skin, evolving up your back. Here
you are, glowing. Incandescent.

The mountain where I met her

Writhe and wrestle and shiver and shed,
slip out of stories and sink slow into the dance floor.
Here, where we name and gather,
resist and welcome whole
drink the shadow
swallow our undomesticated medicine
walk through the woods while snow falls.

Grief work matters.
So does resistance and unrest.
So does love.

Hiraeth

He picked it out, the hat, when we were driving through some unnamed town, stopping for gas and groceries. He picked it out and we paid for it and we wore it out of the store. And I said, "Oh, I love it. It's like Holden Caulfield's hunting cap, but black." And then he asks me why I'm crying. And I say, "You haven't read it yet. But you will. It's about wanting to save your sibling, and not being able to. So in some ways, it's about love. And growing up. Like you will. You will grow up." And he says, "But I don't have brothers and sisters," and I say "Yes, but you will love people. And it's the most amazing thing, isn't it, how reading certain books can change your life. That's how it was for me." And he says, "I wonder if it's the it's the same as writing them."[5]

[5] what changes in a year:

for you

Thank you for your secrets and your proud declarations and
your quiet whispers and your looks of
unquestioning outrage.
Thank you for your anger and your clarity and your confusion
and your raw grief, even all these years later.
Thank you for your anger, your elegant wrists of unspoken,
your lived stories.

I am saying thank you.
I am saying your voice matters.
I am saying I believe you.

passage

love and bodies. determination
and the indescribable unknown.
what a brutal and magnificent way to
come into this world.[6]

[6] birth

parallel lives

All day yesterday, I kept feeling the pull back,
tugging at the sharp parts of my body.
All day today I have stood here, opened like a hymnal spilling
sounds I know without knowing,
tumbling through the skin's memory, traveling
reckless and gossamer veins.[7]

[7] liminal space

wisdom

To cease the war inside.
To love the dark passage.
To crush hard on the comfort of loving the woman
I worked to become and set free.
To ride the wild horse.
To un-name the given gods, harsh velvet on the tongue.
To hear confession and hold the hurt and
know what I will never speak.
To welcome want.
To fight hard and love harder.

wading water over my head

In ancient Greece, as found in the Hippocratic Corpus, the womb in the female body was considered to be ravenous, desperate and devouring, always in search of fulfillment, filled beyond full. I always felt that as belonging to my heart, to its legion ways. How sometimes it feels hungry, feels like a hunter, feels like the terrible exposure of its pulpy beating might be my undoing.
But the womb? My womb? It wanted to be left alone. And what do you do then, with all the times it was not?

here all dwell free

It turns out, my life had always belonged to me.[8]
And so when I walked into the unhinged,
undone house of my heart, it didn't yell at me for having left,
for having wanted to do unthinkable things.
It just said welcome home.

---

[8] and this was the unlocking with my own keyed arm and hand

the completeness of you

Do not ask your wilderness to be a cultivated rose garden.
Do not ask your untamed to be domicile.
Do not ask your honey sweetness to be bitter dark, or your
emptied hollows to be food for others,
or your bones to trade places with your veins.[9]

They are, all of them,
already all yours.

[9] for integration is not merger.

gratitude

To the one who told me no. Thank you.
To the one who tended to the wounds. Thank you.
To the one who stood there while I cooked dinner and pressed
thin filo dough onto parchment paper and baked baklava,
and then spoke into the silence. Thank you.
To the one who ran into the woods with me. Thank you.
To the one who let me get away. Thank you. Thank you.
Thank you.

against all odds

How do we ever find the ways through?
How do we survive?
How we do we keep making art and meaning and love?

I want some smart answer, some clear concise page to
pull from the volumes that tell us where the promise
sinks teeth into the disbelieving,
but I own nothing so lovely.
I have, rather, this. Only this:

Everything is always dying and
someone somewhere is being born.
In all this, a thing so wildly vast,
you are like no other that has ever existed.
How stunning. How magnificent. How much, you matter.
I love you. I love you. I love you.

CONSECRATE

[**kon**-si-kreyt]

verb

1. to make or declare worthy, life's messy and profane magnificence.
2. to set apart, mark as an object or moment of honor.
3. to devote oneself to that which gives life.
4. to ingest the forbidden, open the closed, see in the dark.
5. to anoint or smear with oil and love all that which you once tried to outrun.

surviving

some kind of reckoning;
this slow rapture, this mess of wonder,
dark and sweet like late summer plums.
i am standing in the thunder
and gardens grow in the ashes,
smoke rising.

unholding the hurt things

Sometimes I take griefs and the
unresolvable unanswerable things
and I tie them to imaginary arrows and send them out to sea,
to rocks raised up like walls of wailing,
sturdy and willing to be worn by water.

And then the light comes in the leaving
and everything, for those brief and true moments,
goes gold.

eve

Life is so very short. There is no time to waste. Bang down the doors of your own true knowing. Smash your own heart with fists of flowers. Wish them freedom and fill your mouth with truth and kindness. Love first your own hunger and your wisdom and your unknowns, and never look back.

in leaving she loved

Old stories, re-told and re-imagined,
hearing her begin to speak.
The portals are everywhere. The beginning has begun.
There is so much we must leave and lose,
if we are ever to know our own names.[10]

[10] Susan speaks

I'd rather live in sin

Ink leaked on skin.
Walking around while talking aloud to ideas
and intimate inanimate objects,
an open pen tapped against collarbone to create the cadence
that becomes the net
that catches the words waiting to arise.
Eating slow bite by bite,
lying on the floor, the hard and held of solid ground,
a nervous system rewiring.

Our art needs substance and humanizing punches of
reality and radical reconnection,
but what if it does not require starving or walking over
burning coals to prove our point of view,
pounding away under the numb of the drink
and the rage of being wronged, the idolization of love
shattering us to obliteration, the stress and strain of
unrelenting hours, no space in sight for lost time and slow time
and detours and unexpected open doors.

There will be no gold stars at the end of this life given out for
how much we suffered,
denied ourselves or displaced our desire.
So maybe we can make mess after mess,
and say no when we want,
and let bare feet touch sand as soon as possible and
find that it is here when our truest work begins.
Because the work is good. And it matters, deeply.

real

love.
her.[11]

[11] answers to the questions that live beyond language

new moon in scorpio

Thin veils and ancient voices
raucous in its readiness, silky in its cry:
come, come, whoever you are.
We could crash a party, slip out of old skin,
burn bright or smolder slow.
We could re-write and wrangle the shadows;
we could drink the moon's emergence and be kind.

Name your numinous, she said to me.
Be patient, she said, for it takes a long time.
Trust most your own experience
and consider that you might learn, in every language.

conversations with water

When hungry, eat food and freedom and unafraid sun.
When tired, sleep. And sleep and sleep and sleep.
When weighted with what you have lost and will never resolve,
loosen your armored limbs and be held in the waves you come from and will return to,
water big enough to hold what a heart cannot.
When not sure what comes next, choose the place and piece of land that speaks what is most real
and listen, which is love.

Wake to waiting words,
thick and dark and sugar skull sweet.
Meet strangers. Tend to your own inner multitudes.
Claim what needs not be spoken,
slay with the wreckage of understanding.
Know who and what you will never leave.
Worship warmth. Sleep in rain. Smell the green
deep of jungle. Watch salt give you back your own self,
wandering and welcoming.

ni putas, ni santas—sólo mujeres

There is, sometimes, a compulsion to clean up the stories after the fact. A revisionist history. To tell a neater, sanitized, commercially popular and sellable story.[12]

[12] Tell the most real story instead:

the way through, wandering

Planes, trains, and automobiles. Walking in the dark. Midnight mass. Waking holy sites. Elvis music on the radio. Candlelight processions. Hard cries. Cold water and kiss of Mary. Feast of French food. And pizza in a hotel bed. A sweater coat that looked and felt like a soft bathrobe, which you wore everywhere. Strong cologne. So many languages. Sweetness. Trees dressed in rosaries. Ave Maria. And then home again.

Lost, and freed in this.[13]

[13] Lourdes

salt + honey

talking in the hotel swimming pool,
the night he turned eleven

"Do you think we only get to be here once?" he asks.
"Yes," I say. "I think just once. One life."
"Me too," he says, "but nobody actually knows."
"Yes. Nobody knows. But there is still maybe more than one chance, even in one life," I say.
"Fair," he says.
"But don't you think the really amazing thing is. I mean, if this is the only time we both get to be here in the world, out of all the chances, we both decided to be here at the same time?
That makes us lucky, I think,
in the one time."
"Yeah, it's like science," he says,
how people find what they need for evolution."
"Yes, like that," I say. "Like art."

fter the fall

Learn the language for hydrangeas, and sovereignty,
and the dark wonder of bats flying against rough stone and
clear water of a cenote named stars and woman.
Make a religion of your contradictions,
make a nest of your broken parts and
become a place you come home to.
Move your hips like the shape eights make,
and bend your back to love the hollow space, and
rush the blood to solid ground.
Say what you mean.
Be reverent and ruthless with the finality of some things,
goodbye, since it must be so.
Say yes to the soft of feathers,
and the curve of a shoulder and your open mouth.
Ask for understanding.

You have survived so much.
You have loved beyond the edge of the scar where the scalpel
and the mountain and the memory collide.
You have woken in the first light and found the oldest stories
on the insides of eyelids and chosen
to open and to see and to drink hot coffee on a porch where
you once came to meet her in your camo pants and high heels,
leaned over to kiss what came next.
You have lost what can never be returned, have had taken
what was essential, watched as the train pulled away and you
remained, which was to leave, and this was life.
And here you still stand. Here you slip into new skin,
and listen to the night, and bite down hard.

geography

Learning the word no;
what it means,
how it feels in the body-arms out,
a clear outline, shape of mine and not mine.

In the quiet and slow heat, falling into easy rhythm with the
want of yes, how it comes all on its own,
lucid and unguarded,
with skinned knees and handfuls of violets.[14]

[14] consent

fault line

When hurting, grow things in the dark of dirt,
peace and bulbs with paper skin.
When not knowing what to do or how to pray or
where to find sense in the senseless,
lay it down,
dance instead.
When life is lost and taken, grieve.
When sleep won't come, create constellations of
meaning from secrets and stars,
and curve your belly to the hushed beauty of her back,
whisper the names to the night.

tell me

What is the color for something part protest, part joy, part
refusal to stay silent?
What is the color for "Yes. Please. Come. Be with me"
and for stay up late and dance into the night and don't forget
what your skin already speaks?
What is the color for a thing
part celebration, part subversive rebellion,
part steady remembrance that we were here?

Habitation

That was the day I decided to be visible.
To occupy my own space, fully.
To inhabit my own heart, wholly.
To show up, drink bitter coffee, open
my eyes, and not be afraid.

you must remember this

Love is plants in every shade of green,
is absence of what was slowing killing you,
is his face when he pulled back the curtain and saw the
lanterns lit over snow below.
Love is the table in which there is always room
and the bruise from blood drawn, which is the reminder
of the body, which is the love that has never left you.

It is knowing who your emergency contact is.
It is not being asked to be what you are not.
It is a life raft stitched together with
red thread and your hedonistic heart.

Love is the moment of doing laundry, and the sheets
billowed out onto the bed and the smallest of sea shells that
must have been in a pocket that then made its way to the
wash that then tumbled into sheets and then there it sat,
some kind of reminder to a love that lets you be when and
where you need to because it trusts always in the return.

I am always making my way back to you.[15]

---

[15] You, Mexico.

"You didn't come into this world. You came out of it,
like a wave from the ocean. You are a not a stranger here."
– Alan Watts

The ground will hold you.
The sky will meet you.
The mountains will tell you how evolution and collisions create the most beautiful things.

two truths

1. Taking the word "maybe" out of the vocabulary and deciding to just decide

   (Yes. No. I want to. I don't want to.)

   is like finding all this unexpected unknown time. All the time that is spent in the stuck of "I don't know. Maybe. Maybe not," is now liberated to the doing and loving of things, to good work, to being here all the way.

2. You are allowed to change your mind.

in the flesh

There are all these things that are real-
the feelings, with their weight and wordless rush and rise in
the body breathing, the unknowns, with their tall shadows and
waiting restless for solid landing.
The questions, the conversations
(talk real to me)
the peaches and pepper of red radishes,
the nap with thick dreams of worlds you could walk into,
returned, the flannel and blue work shirt and soft sweater.
The fears, the art asking to happen,
the unexpected move and madness of all things colliding.
The memories I never wanted to re-remember.
The other ones too, of dried flowers and tinctures,
a girl of a woman saving herself.
The way birds fly in gatherings, and the splendor and
ache of this, or how my chest feels like someone is pressing
down, making it hard to breathe,
the soft of feather beds,
the way we break and still keep walking.

Sometimes what is real feels like the arrow and the wound
and the way out, all at once.
And then this. If all these things are here and true,
so too is this what is real-
this slip of light coming down upon roaring water,
this hint of pink and opened crack where an ending came to
shatter out its last embers and how it will happen again
tomorrow and tomorrow, and how tonight,
all the real things came to bear witness.

atlas of heat

Clay and honey clover and cool metal. The way grief stains paper and minds, leaving marks that alter the atlas of everything that comes after. The sound of so many birds, pounding and flapping feathered beats inside the lining of the heart. The way the truck tires sound on dirt, when it is late and liquid and the air is thick as want. Life force. Homeopathy. So you don't need to tell me, that my medicine is poison. I already know. That's why it works. The statue of Aphrodite with the cross they came and scarred into her forehead. Metrics of splendor. Memory of when we had wings.[16]

---

[16] What does it feel like, she asked me.
This, I said.
What, she said.
Fire, I said. I'm on fire.

today's shopping list

two lemons
postage stamps
liquid ink
steak
fishnets
hellebore
blackberries for pie

where do we come from?

The things that change.
The things that remain.
The size nine and a half boots.
The inability to remember in the womb.
The evergreen. The sap on skin.
The face I keep staring at, in memory and in
honest unknown.[17]

---

[17] My son at eleven.

close to the bone

When everything was cold, and the relief would not come. When we didn't know how we would survive. When we ate strawberries by the basket full and I left secret messages on the steamed window while sitting in salt water baths. When I made dream maps on the floor underneath my bed, and protested in the streets, and made art of smoke and wings. When I knew it was all the way over, and I would never look back, and how I didn't know how afraid I had been all the time, until that moment; how I didn't understand how complicated it had been, to love what hurts.

The year of driving the pacific coast alongside pounding ocean and into canyons, singing open. And moonshine, and bare legs. How you took so much, from my clamped hands and my restless release. How you left presents at my doorstep. How you don't care the way we think you should, and how I somehow love you for this, for your willingness to be Life. The year of water words, of footnotes and the mystery and space between things, and waking to the rushing sound and how I knew then I was going to make it. The year of understanding the unbearable cost of survival. Of gold bracelets and walking back to say please let me kiss you. The year I wrote on my own skin and ate watermelon while sitting on the kitchen floor late at night, free.

When I learned to read the bones. When I wore again whatever I wanted and said no all the time. (The year I came and left. The year I slept alone.)
Where nothing is forbidden and nothing left out.[18]

---

[18] The year my life belonged to me.

silver stag

After the gray of wait and cold concrete
finally, then,
the falling of snow and full moon.

intimate shadows

The body that shows the topography of injuries,
knows a want like hunger and cannot bear to be touched
lightly but only strong and sure, the way you might
press down hard to try to stop the bleeding.
The haunting of hunting season and the hallowed spaces
where you dug out the decay with bruised fists and the way
sometimes still, even after all these years, you still feel the way
two o'clock tastes on the mouth, filled with broken conquests
and heat from the concrete
and somewhere in the space where shoulder blades attempt
to touch in the chest opening,
you still miss it.

The never being able to quite find the right language to say
what really happened.
The wanting the relief of not having to explain.
The nightmares that never leave.
The reckless glory of a waterfall washing over you,
the sound of it like a roar, and the way she brought you coffee
in bed and the plant that hung there in the shower, spilling
down like there was still time enough for everything that came
after.

The scars that formed on the inside of skin, intimate and
devastating, invisible to the rushing world.

body language

To the pulse in the lip, that says come closer.
To the burn on the top of my hand,
stretched like secret translations.
To the hunger (for waffles. for heat. for art. for the bridge of Frida's house).
To the fear in my throat and the murmur of wet skin.
To the hurt hip and the slow Sunday, and the
restless of waiting and the surrender to love for
the body that speaks.[19]

---

[19] *Listen.*
Ok, I said.
I'm listening.

impossible possible

It could happen. You know this, right?
You could lay down your swords and kiss your scars and
make altars of you wrecked and insistent fate line,
make a bed of rosewater and skin,
make a home of hard laughter and second acts and your need
to find and be found.

leaving my father's house

You will never understand what happened those years.
And at some point in time, it will be ok
to let go of the need to know,
and tell your own story.

think in ways you've never thought before

1. Think that at any moment, of any day, you could be walking down the street, taking a short cut through the alley, or passing by familiar store fronts, and see a door you have never noticed before, and when you walk inside, there in front of you is the thing that changes everything, a whole new world.
2. That there is enough. That if you spend it all, giving everything you have, on what is here, right now, a kind of abandon, there will be more tomorrow, and the next day, and the next.
3. That all the maps were wrong.
4. That maybe Cinderella took off her glass slipper because she didn't want to wear uncomfortable shoes anymore, or Sleeping Beauty just decided to take a nap because she was tired. Or Persephone made a choice, not victim, because something in her was hungry for the underworld. Or what Pandora found when she opened the box was nothing like anything that has ever been written, and she didn't feel sorry about it, ever.
5. Think that the universe is indifferent and still somehow benevolent. That nothing is important, and everything matters.
6. That you are not her, or him. That you don't really know, what's it like to be her, in her reality.
7. That the person you have spent so much time disagreeing with could be the one who shows you the way.
8. Think that what you always assumed was backwards, back doors, was in fact the front. That everything can be turned around. or upside down. That direction is not static.
9. That the weight of all the problems does not always rest on you. You are not so important. And that all of this, this whole world, is here and was made for you.
10. That even if they never understand, it is still ok.
11. That you could be understood, without saying a word.

12. Think that the tree you once climbed as a child, knew as shelter and adventure cry, that it was once planted by someone who didn't know you, but still, in some way, placed the seed in the ground for you.
13. That the thing you spent years running from will become your closest companion and kindest teacher.
14. That just because "this", the thing or way or system, is the way it's always been done, doesn't mean you have to do it that way. Now. Or ever.
15. That the reoccurring dream could come to completion by another. And the imaginary friend you prayed to in childhood turned out to be real, and you found one another. And you would never be all the way alone again.
16. Think that if you had x-rays done, the slides up on the light board, black and white and gray, would show a tiger in your ribcage, hieroglyphics on your pelvis, an unknown language running up your spine, lilacs tumbling out of your clavicle.
17. Think that children could be teachers. And words used as weapons could be walked away from. And you could wake up in the morning and find an entire opera or mathematical formula or cookbook had come to you in your sleep. And who you once were would not feel abandoned or threatened, but just be happy, for who you have become

ɿrned; loving those in the dying

If there is someone you want to talk to, pick up the phone. Show up at the door (Even after all these years. Even if it seems reckless. Even if you don't know what comes next. Especially if you don't know what comes next). Say what you need to say. Ask them the question. Let the answer liberate, in one direction or another, or maybe in every way, all directions, stretched wide.

Your experience is your own. You are allowed it.
The fullness of it. The complexity and contradiction of it.
The brazen intimacy of it. You are not required to explain or defend it. It is yours, belonging to you, true.

It is alright to leave.

Let the water hold you. Let the ground meet you and carry you. Let the sky crack open in front of you.

Do not die not knowing what their mouth tastes like, or what those mountains would feel like in front of you, or with words left writhing inside you.

Feed yourself.

We are human. We have needs. Desire, yes. But also tender and terrible and achingly human needs. Meeting each other, face to face, speaking needs, allowing another to meet them and to reach out and meet theirs, is one of the most powerful experiences we get to have as human animals.

If you have hurt or harmed someone, if you are sorry, say you are sorry. And also, your life, your personhood, does not require an apology for existing, being here, human.

Not all things are equal, or fair. We do not come into the world on a level playing field. And we do not all make it, recover, get better, heal, thrive. And it is not because we didn't punch in the right formula in the positive thinking machine. Life is often hard, and deeply painful, and embedded in violence that we build our very lives upon. So we just don't know, if it will all be ok, what, if any, meaning we will come to make of it. But what *is* possible, is to let go the arrogance of claiming to know what another knows or needs or experiences in their own skin, and then show up opened and emptied, listening as if your own life depended upon it. Because it does.

Memory is not fixed or static.
Neither are our hearts.
Neither is the ocean.

Art can change the world.

When scared, when things feel complicated, when not knowing how or when the next breath will come, bringing things deeply into the most bare space can be the most extravagantly beautiful thing possible. Drinking a glass of water. Seeing your reflection in a mirror and finding your twelve-year-old self. Screaming secrets. Hands. Shoulders. Hold me, please. See me. Tell me I was here. Remind me what is real. Please. Thank you.
I love you.

in her skin

I love you the way you love a wild thing,
not meant to be tamed.
I love you the way you love your origin myth,
your beginnings, the salt
water womb from which you once came.
I love you, as I love the heart you house,
having your back, webbed in ribcage.
I love you as home, and as that which takes me to the edge of
adventure and risk and welcome breaking open.
I love you whole, complete.

You, this web of cells and memory and feeling,
bone and blood and heat
my house of belonging
my way of knowing
my resting place and my wrestling space.
I love you.[20]

---

[20] to the good body, my body.

the sweetness of downfall

I sit in conversation with colleagues,
read and study and write about religious revelation.
I take notes, consider questions,
know none of it as belonging to me.

But outside the ideas of right and wrong,
in the place where freedom lives.
Outside the walls that house words. Outside is the silver and
gold glow, forever changing, forever returning, hidden and
revealed,
new and full. Always whole.
And whatever god is or is not, if anything at all,
there is you.
And you're the honey and the moon.

grief

noun

1. not at all like I thought it would look like.

2. a thing far more inclusive, polarizing, untamed and quiet and complete.

3. how it happens at night in the bathtub. and in the wrestling. and in the smallest of things, like looking both ways before crossing the street.

your hands and my skin

To unearth the scar stories and the trembling in ecstasy stories and the quiet vibrations that rippled out over everything the moment when you understood that everything was connected and you didn't have to figure any of it out. You could just be here, alive, in love.[21]

---

[21] This is the map of the flesh,

querencia

To be aware, awake,
when your life is in the moment of changing
and to know in this how all the lines connected,
converging into this, here, now.
Hidden wholeness ripped open like revelation.

the hurt of healing

Ridges of raised white. Slashes on the back.
Unspoken tellings.
Violence and accident and illness.
Flashes of sight and insight.
Childhood in the haze of summer, and mountains running.

What happened. What we tell ourselves. The imagined and the unexpected. Life. All that life happening.
The one who gave them.
The one who read them.
Wisdom of the body.
Topography of skin.[22]

[22] story of scars

all the real vows

Standing there this morning, coffee cup in one hand and with the other hand trying to tie my hair up in a knot around a pen. Standing there, feet in the middle of a mandala of last night's dress on the floor with the piles of books and left out water glasses and ink stains. Hearing the sound of the train, and knowing it's time to leave and stopping ever so quickly to look again at the note cards sprawled with words in constellations on the wall, and stopping all the way, slow and drenched, to kiss and listen for the pulsing heartbeats finding one another. It was one of those moments when everything was quiet and ravished and illuminated.

Sometimes it seems like lots of voices are yelling at me to love myself, a clamoring demand for the performance of self-acceptance. So I have to go be in my life without anyone else's ideas for a while. Then all on its own, this morning, it was just one of those moments, extravagant and unkempt, smeared with everything real, when I looked around and knew the meaning of my love. And it was presence and trust that I could build a life on.

Maybe we don't have to try so hard. Maybe we can just be here and choose not to abandon ourselves, even when we don't like ourselves. Maybe this is the way to unlocking our own desire, and our desire is a wisdom that we can follow like winged migration, knowing it will take us as far away as we need in order to land in our home, the sanctuary of heart, the flesh where we claim amnesty for the internal torment and body divided. I don't know for certain, but this is how it was for me. And so it is a mystery and an honoring of every time I placed myself in the head of the dragon and learned to breathe fire, that this morning was just a morning. Except it was everything, every moment that had lead up to now, all of it alive.

And I thought, this needs its own word, this moment,[23] inexplicably falling in love with my own cracked and surviving self, with life in all its evolution and unholy beauty.

---

[23] Communion:

milk and honey

And just like that everything seemed somehow possible.[24]

[24] to a full moon

denouement

Refuse to live at war with your own self
and flesh and ancient
ocean of emotion.
Surrender to the living
collecting your bone stories,
making sentences and sailboats and love.

taking back the year that the locusts have eaten

You were the great taking and the reparation.
You were the way I learned what it is to not leave myself,
to simply stay, and how this is what I had, my whole life,
wanted the most.
You were late nights at the gym, boxing shadows and bags, and
you were waking to the curve of her back and coffee in bed.
You[25] were work destroyed and art reborn,
my path uncrossed and set clear,
my devotion an offering at the altar of the living and dying.

And thank you. For all of this.
For coming. For now leaving.
For the ways you delivered completion and the way you
broke the rules and brought me to here.
The horses have pounded their way against
salt water and sand, and they just dropped me off here in my
apartment of antlers and broken glass and wings,
geranium and new notebooks and the shelter of
no longer waiting.
They told me that I'm good now, free to go live my life.
I love you too, I said. True story.

---

[25] the year I had cancer for the second time,

recipe for pulling down the moon

- mix a handful of rose water with a broken locket of grief, a persimmon sliced open and the smell of the book stacks, and call it your secular baptism.

- take coarse salt and orchid and smooth them over your skin before slipping into paper wings.

- do not harm the dark. do not let go the light.

- love your hard laughter. flex your feet. taste ocean. tell me the worst thing you've ever done and watch how the world still wakes and my table names you as belonging.

- show mercy. claim pleasure as your birthright.

- sit in waiting rooms. slow time. the tck, tck, tck, tck of a wall clock and the quiet voices behind tall tables and the rustle of paper against soft shoulders on the other side of the wall. the television tells of rage, and the fragility of emptiness. watch. pay attention. wonder at the performance of prevention, how we pretend we can beat a thing before it begins. let yourself love her, with all of you known and unknown.

- fill your mouth with what mends and let your hands feel your own flesh, cells formed from stardust and lust and the radical ground that gave you life.

COMMUNION

[k*uh*-**myoon**-y*uh* n]

noun

1. interchange or sharing of thoughts and emotions.
2. receiving the elements in the forest or the ocean or the el train late at night when the tracks spark bright light into the restless dark.
3. the act of sharing: ourselves, what we have, what we need.
4. the state of things so held.
5. intimacy.

coming

You are the poem and you are the prayer.
You are the question and you are the innate knowing.

Or what about this one, the one I'd bet my
whole hand on, all in.
What if life is a waiting lover, and you already taste the
truth, because you
(yes, you)
are the way.

weather warning

It was all of the sudden,
on my way to the library,
how you could feel the exact moment it shifted.
The air was heavy and sky turned gravel gray,
dark in the late morning,
and the smell of storm came over everything.
Within minutes it was raining hard and
the low growl of thunder was its own wordless language.

Now.
Now I am sitting out on my covered back steps.
Now it is pouring.
And I'm thinking how both loss and love are this way too.
How sometimes they come quiet,
slow and black cherry sweet.
How sometimes they come like a tempest,
like a sudden crossroads, like a Midwestern thunderstorm,
crashing and beautiful.

lilacs

even if it means barbed wired wound around rib cage to
protect what pounds.
even if it is asking questions that have no answers.
even if unknotting is the undoing.
whatever it takes to stay soft,
do that.

directions

Reverence for the profane and scared scars of the body.
Holding my own flesh like a holy site, a loved map,
an unbound pleasure.

Visitation

Feeling the way the word lucky fills the whole mouth,
tongue against rooftop,
lips opened like the light that pours down in a painting,
washing over Mary right before she hears the news.

Komorebi

There was once a dream I had, half waking half sleeping, of enchanted forests with lights illuminated from trees as if they belonged there, as if skin and bark were meant to be lit up like irrepressible life. And you would have to call this magic, wouldn't you? I mean if you stumbled upon it, while out walking through woods. You would falter in your lack of faith wouldn't you, doubt at your doubt, disbelieve your disbelief? You would wonder if you were dreaming, or how it is possible to have never known until this moment,

awakening.

And last night, listening to her talk of dreamt places, maps known and returned to, summer sun making music in its rustling cadence through branches and onto water. Last night, listening
to her, I thought,

I believe, I believe, I believe.

run away home

When I was fifteen, alone, living in Germany,[26] falling in love with freedom, riding a train to Berlin. When I drank dark beer at the bar with no name, and stayed up through the night and came upon the waves of tulips breaking into bloom. When I banged against stone with metal pipes and memorized smashed graffiti in my mind.

Where I listened for stories in the streets, country after country, and began to hear the rumbling and rising up of my own. Where I cut all my hair off and watched snow fall high up in the mountains and knew myself as forever a stranger which meant my home was the whole world.

---

[26] two years after the wall fell,

ravel

The way we were laying there, heaved together
at the end of a day,
and I said, "do you like lover more? or love? or beloved?
Which is the better word?”

And she just said, "it's you."

everything that comes after

Did you know when we are born there are two hundred and seventy bones underneath our skin, and then over time, some of them fuse together, into only two hundred and six? Isn't that amazing somehow, that we evolve in that way, the opposite of continental drift? How we are in some way trying to mend something back together, find the forms inside where things finally fit.

Did you know that out of the two hundred and six bones, twenty-seven of them are in your hand? Are in my hand. So much intricate bone for something so small. And I'm looking down at my hands, and wondering of the names of the bones beneath the skin and anatomical diagrams found on the wall in the not-quite cold doctor's office.

I want to call them moonshine and Venice beach, black ink and credence and Solomon, the wrist called Bathsheba or impermanence or latchkey. This bone is the named "all the shades of white walls" and this over here will be named "the placement of long forgotten things." And maybe the real question is, why, if I'm writing of the bones in my hands, can I only think of the ladder of her side, rising up and down to heartbeat. "You have the most beautiful rib cage I've ever seen," I said, and then had a moment of pulling back, aware of the strangeness of the sounds of the words. Except its true. The bones of them, the elegance of space between. The exquisite architecture, of her.

I would name it redemption, and how my own hands would reach out and touch the ladder of her, again and again and again.

( )

you. the meaning that lives beyond words.

homeopathy

My skin that softens and my legs that open and
my jaw and shoulder blades that come un-clenched
whenever summer comes.
My doors.
My history and stories and the way they never truly leave
but instead mark and map me, and the
willingness to still leave them behind and start new.
My scars and the stretched spaces.

Myself. I belong to myself.

salt + honey

brick by brick
breath by breath

I am building a home from my contradictions.

come home to me, in twenty words or less

heavy rain. hot bath. cold cream pie.
violets and words crashed together at just
the right moment.
thinking of you.

recovery

What it feels like, when the grief heaves you out of
the belly of the whale,
tosses you to shore.
What it tastes like: the kiss, the mouth, even as you still
remember the feel of sand sticking to skin
while you pulled seaweed from your hair.

Miles

Together.
Which is sometimes side by side, or closer even,
when he sits next to me and pinches my arm and we eat
cold pasta straight from the to-go carton.
Which is sometimes homes or miles apart,
our own worlds, separate and still threaded through with
the us that began the moment I first saw him.
Which is sometimes at odds or
mixed up misunderstanding and sometimes the contentment
of standing next to one another while the city speeds by and
no words need to be said
because there is no question.
We are together.
Mother and son. Separate and
forever bound.

reunion

We left what we were doing and came, to honor a friend who died in a way we can't make any sense of and so the numb and the hurt and the ravages of grief all overlap and make unsuspecting shapes of things, like contorted hands turning into shadow ships and animals on the wall. It is love we've spent twenty years making. Nothing turned out the way we thought it would. We keep wanting to say the true things, and in the end we have only the real things. So we make blankets and mosaics with them, pieces patched together. And we stand there, wrapped up, staring at beauty we could not have seen coming, any more than we could predict the loss.

fidelity

I love her. It is that simple, and complete,
stripped down to real, met in shadows and roaring light,
adorned with Milagros and anatomical heart art and the
pleasure of solitude
and the electricity of return.

All the words only work as arrows,
trying to point toward the way.
But the love is the way,
and I love her.

letters smashed together

Their timelessness, walking us from one life to the next. All the ones written on my walls, and how as I think about moving, I wonder which ones will be left behind, and what new ones will come find me one day when I'm walking in from the rain to get a hot coffee and pick up the newspaper that has the sentence that changes everything. How one day when I will be in the wrecks of grief and have no god to turn to, I'll wander the cramped aisles of the used book store, scouring poetry for a language to meet me where I am. One day, I will be sitting on the el and see the banner poster that has graffiti, and know in that moment what I was always waiting for. I don't know what they will be. Only that yes, they will come.[27]

[27] the importance of words

love child

I am the love child of red riding hood and the wolf
of Bob Dylan and Lois Lane
of henna dye and seaweed.
Hestia and Hecate
the hunter and the hunted
tequila and turpentine.

I am the love child of Psyche and Eros
of walked wilderness and unspoken wild
of alley cat and Frida Kahlo, antlers and burlesque, defiance
and soft feathers
cartography and skin.

Legion heart.
Love and beloved.

remember

I would cross the bridges,
all of them
again and again,
every time, in every life,
to walk with you in this world.

before speech

Open, unwavering, to the outrage and the sublime.
Observant as worship and blood as war and
quiet as the white breath coming from the mouth in the
frozen cold of winter.

I have nothing smart to say
or simple enough to fit inside the sounds of syllables
but

last night I fell asleep to the sound of rain and thunder.
This morning I woke to my hieroglyphic heartbeat,
the crash of breaking things and beginning things,
all of it is some kind of language.

I am baptized in listening.

David

My grandpa. The texture of his hands,
rough but soft palmed.
The way he insisted upon my happiness as if it mattered.
The worn pages of his books.
His gravel voice that only ever spoke kindness to me.
The feel of lifesavers passed from hand to hand down the pew while we all sat there at church,
and how he never ran out, his candy seeming to multiply like loaves and fishes.

breaking the spell

"It's not pretty," I say,
describing my state of unhinged, unkempt
diving off the deep end. My discomfort,
the rough around the edges and raw.

"It is interesting, isn't it," she says, "that women are so conditioned in this culture to follow up words of wildness and anger with - it's not pretty - as if it somehow always should be, and we have broken the rules."[28]

---

[28] beauty standards

eyes first opened

What would happen if we sat in front of other people with full presence, and believed that the embodied self could be read like books? Would we fall at the feet of their poetry? Would we be willing to be surprised, and educated, and amazed? Would we cry when we had to get up and leave, because everyone knows that sometimes, it's the last page that is the hardest?

rise up rooted

The trees.
They were my first home.
And flight of freedom.
And keeper of my stories.

partnered

Intimacy born of an honoring for what is distinctive,
and deep love for the rooting together, the mad urge to
run reckless and whole
into an unknown and say "You. This. I'm all in."
Space, even as the stems intertwine at base and the
leaves so green they still remember the jungle of their
once ago origin.

They say orchids need just the right conditions to grow.
Not the sturdiest; unable to thrive in any climate.
But maybe asking for what we need is what makes us strong,
able to open
like a body giving over to heat.
Maybe this is why I love them.
My own shadow, known in white and purple petals,
wanting and wanting and wanting
and when met, a cascade of
stunning, unapologetic beauty.

evolution

Bones wrapped in embroidered flowers.
Heart the size of Mexico and her.
Protection worn as if it were possible to see inside,
As if an X-ray illuminated not just what is there,
but what comes next.
As if the light board would show Maggi wandering and dogs
searching and a tropical forest thick with heat.

There is this question. There is this blur of a moment.
(What if this is all love really is?)
What if you don't have to push yourself into the future, she
asked. *What if it is already arrived, and is, even now, pulling
you forward?*
Which is the saddest and most beautiful thing possible,
the way life wants to happen, stopping for nothing.

imbrication

I forgive myself for not having been able to stop what happened. I forgive myself for loving clumsily and with a need that devoured. I forgive myself for not being able to make better what was broken from the moment I breathed. I forgive myself for wanting and trying and falling and flailing. I forgive myself for there not being do overs and changed histories and for what it felt like to pull my body from the cave, and sprawl my limbs upon grass, and walk the aisle, and pull the needle from my arm, and break the vows, and kiss the open hand. Even without guilt there is the impulse toward the confession that craves our own forgiveness. "And what does it even mean?" I hear shudder around inside me, as if even my own language will betray my contradictions.

So let's just say this:
Take out the word forgiveness.
In its place land the word love.
Say it all again.

city of ruins

saltwater heart.
frida's daughter heart.
origami heart, corners turned in toward each other,
kinked and bent into something beautiful.
heart the size of a continent and an intimate room,
glowing neon, a tangle of seaweed and dark boxes and
smooth stones, beloved.
lungs of secret handshakes and moon rivers
and that which is claimed.

(breathe. with me.)

bones of heat and consequence.
curved calf of things lost and found.
body. of water and of words and of heart beats, pounding and
murmuring sweet.
smeared kohl and parted lips.
razor blade questions and knowing what you truly need
and ink, spilled, the color of indigo, of ocean.

safe house

Storms rage outside and inside we make shelter
of paper ships to sail away on,
windows and worlds of pages and ink.[29]

[29] refuge in words

invisible ink

In the morning, in the wave of missing,
in the waking wrapped up in twists
of sheets and dreams of plastic beads and Spanish moss
hanging loose from trees.
In the getting up to make coffee and coming back,
reaching over toward notecards and pen so as to
write the remains.
And catching, then, the sight of things left,
the memory that comes, the land of particulars,
the look on her face when she unclasped the earrings and set
them beside the bed.

We say the word love and it's the crashing wave of so
much, the meaning almost lost in the largeness.
When really, the love seems often the details of things.
How she arches her feet when extending her
legs in stretch. The slant of her handwriting.
The way her face and true tellings teach me how to trust.
The tilt of her head to the side when taking out the fortune
tellers from her ears,
leaving them likely by accident, to be found and read like a
letter understood only to the writer and receiver.

human

In case you needed to hear it today:

It is ok to not be ok. Because sometimes, it isn't, and the most honoring thing possible is to be fierce with reality.

It is ok to be broken in ways that feel like they might not ever mend, and to fall in love with your scars and to hate them still when the heat changes right before the rain comes. To be so gorgeously lit up that when you walk in a room everyone stares because we all know we've just seen something breathtakingly holy in flesh and red shoes and a human at home inside themselves. It is ok to be quiet. Not everything requires a response. It is ok to not know, and to mess up, to try things, and learn through doing. To be wrong, and realize that, and apologize, and change. It is ok to leave, to alter the agreement, to realize you can no longer keep the vow you once made because you have become someone different in all these lifetimes from that moment years ago, and the most loving thing possible is to know when to stand strong in the truth of a changing woman.

It is ok to grieve. To not know how you will make it through. To not know if you want to. To sell almost everything you own and get lost on a life raft for a while. To lose whole hours and days of your doing to building houses of playing cards, only to have the queen of diamonds land on your lap and know in that moment that you have just opened the door to the other side.

To thrash and to throw up armor and to abandon your nice and release your now worn strategies. To dream again, and to dive into the deep water and scream.

To trust your gut and to doubt your decisions. To be so filled with paradoxes that you become the most beautiful thing any of us has ever seen. To wink at the couple walking by and choose to go to bed alone. To make out and make up and marry your own heart still beating.

To like yourself. To love yourself. To not get to control how the story ends. It is ok, to be here, human in this world. And more than ok, I think it is what we are here to do. And for this, I love you.

in the beginning

When the air starts to turn and blow wild through
open windows, threatening to storm downpour.
When, even as papers start blowing off walls and table,
the candles stay lit and feel like the lamppost in the
wardrobe, lighting the way.
When Mary starts talking to you in matchsticks and your
heart feels like it's made of beating wings
and cracked walls and blue iris.
When you are homesick and in love
and you sit down and write.

And then it is two hours later, and you have pages
stacked on top of each other and none of the words
may make sense, but they are all yours.
And it starts to rain and you think "Yes, perhaps I
understand in my own way what it means. . .
the word became flesh.

refuge

I am an open border.
And if the world makes barriers,
I will come to you, with everything I have.

her

I was once a girl of a woman with smoke
and secrets in my lungs,
with terror and defiance and dark purple
smudged around my eyes,
and for those years I knew only the names for survival.

This too was a kind of love.

Hecate

When the heart has cracks in the concrete that happened
so many years ago, and every opening now feels like
every loss you've ever known might come pulsing out the
lower left quadrant.
When this beckoning is all you've ever wanted.
When the woodpecker lives in your rib cage.
When only the woods will do.

for you

Life is often hard, and the most horrible things happen. And we still get up and turn to the ones next to us and say *I love you, I hate you, I want you, I am here,* and then get out of bed and go into a waiting world. We still run hands through hair and get on trains and read interesting books and cook steak dinners and strawberry pie and ignore the odds and bare scars from traumas we could never have avoided. We cannot be immunized from being human.

Still, we are here.
Without a god, I turn to her, my beloved,
I once was lost, but now I'm found
I say.
Thank you, for finding me.

Kansas

After clawing and ripping away at every scrap and shred
of the yellow wallpaper that housed my terror and
the silencing of being told I should sit there and take it and
count myself lucky for surviving.
After tearing away till the fingers bleed,
beating toward the door.
After the unlocking that arrived when
I became my own key.
After all this,
how strange, how wonderful, to stumble upon a field of
wild yellow and fall in love.
To hold the remnant in a hand, and wonder at how it happens.
How madness becomes mystery and you sit
there among cedar trees and listen to your own undoing,
your soft heart, your opened vault of memory.

i am my own[30]

I am fishnets and a wild thing
running through the woods.
I am hard bite and the need to be held by water.
I am loud, and she who wants heavy blankets, and the one
who will never resolve where she came from.
I am clarity of consent and the bare branches
strong enough to swing from.
I am fingers inside the mouth
and the woman whose heart valve grew a garden.
I am shiver and shudder and an ancient cave,
handfuls of orchids and inside me lives hot springs.

I am what happened in the back of pick-up trucks
and what happens when blackberries stain hands and
saltwater saves the slow disappearing.
I am integrated, and shards of glass they never fully removed
from my skin,
a bathtub filled with black sunshine,
heart of devotion, body of a living story.

I am my own.

My name is The kiss on the soft underside of the knee.
My name is angry, and inevitable orphan, and pilgrim.
My name is please, please, please.
My name is heat.
My name is The light that loved the dark.
My name is I believe.

---

[30] Naming my own animals,

twenty-four hour diners and lovers who read fortunes

Sometimes I don't understand how anything works,
or why things fall apart of how they mend.
I just know that there is some kin of kindness,
and I was in the shelter of its wings as it passed over me.

magical surrealism

When I heard you speak, something in me fell out.
Or entered in.
And how was I supposed to perform the ritual of
piecing myself together again,
when all I wanted now was to be pierced,
construction happening only in the act of disruption?

revealed

The only way through this is to love more.
Radical love. Uncomfortable love. Justice love.
Willing to take a stand love. I would die for this love.
I will live for this love.[31]

[31] and this was my liberation.

taking back my life

supplies for starting again:
cold beer
paper and pen
fire escape steps
the sound of summer rain

crush

To the blank page and the blinking cursor. To the words that
want to come and sometimes get stuck somewhere
between imagined and mouth. To the first time I
heard my own language. To the rage that was
released. To the slow and unspectacular,
the messy and earth bound,
the hours of knowing I am
lost and not caring. To the
night. To the typewriter.
To the titles. To the
cadence and the
sound and the
way some words come stark like branches exposed.

To writing.
I love you.

annunciation

The amaryllis bulb waiting to bloom, stalk stems
thick and green, and arced toward winter window light.
The thumping and the tremble and the not knowing.
The face imagined and not yet seen.
The beginning before the beginning.
The wet of fecundity.
The way a body carries us, from one life into the next.
Gestation. Waiting. Roaring love.

liturgy

Disrupt. Dismantle. Tear it all down.
Build, and re-invent the world,
word by word, choice by choice, in exile and embrace,
revolution and revelation, slayed by lovingkindness.

When I sat among sawdust and wood beams

Afterwards,[32] even small things become illuminated for their magnificence and sturdy resiliency.
Like dandelions picked and clutched in the fist, held out as offering. Like how good really cold beer tastes when it is hot outside. Like the wanted haunting permanent ink brings, and the willingness to risk asking for the first kiss, and the return to water.

This is what I know. There is no cure. For anything.
But there is so much life. It is gory and glorious.
And all I can say to her is thank you. I choose you.
All of you.

---

[32] After the brutality of illness,

broken fate line

Unmade bed as invitation.
The need for comfort like wings,
for shelter and for flight.
The way we say open, and assume it's the better option, better
than closed and the contagion of fear that
clamps and confines. Except, my heart and psyche and
even the crashing of my skin,
it just doesn't work this way.
Open, yes. And then close, breathe refuge,
grow deep in the dark, and then open.
Again and again and again.
open. close. open. close,
cadence like hedonistic hymns.
So unmade bed, like invitation.
Come. Stay. Hearts beating strong.

sacrament

If I write my heart, what comes is love for the body.
If I write the curves and scars
and arched instinct of my body,
what comes is the moment when I stand up from the bed
where I've been sprawled with books and paper and bleeding
pens, because the music fills that space
between spine and cupped pelvic bone,
compels me to dance, and so the voice is the
language of movement,
which is pleasure, with is protest, which is joy.
If I move to the language of my dance, I belong to no man,
no woman, no deity, no dogma. I am my own.
If I speak from the lightning of my own belonging, then my
solid ground is ashes anointed with outcast waters
and the throat opens, welcomed like finding the question
finally, for the answer you heard all those years ago
and mistook for evacuation.
It wasn't banishment; it was pointing the way back in.

I love, the heart and flesh that welcomes home.

missed connections

When I walked into the room for coffee, the room with those vaulted industrial loft ceilings and the exposed brick that broke off in your hands, I could not stop turning toward you. Because my back felt arched a new direction and my tongue now tasted like sun, and I could not bear how hungry and beautiful it was, the things that would follow. The blond of your hair, mostly matted, and the sundresses and sneakers you wore without shoe laces, and the shape of your hands pouring water over your legs. The cookies you made with too much butter. The recklessness of want. The terrible grief of finding what we need when we cannot yet say yes. And I wanted, so much, to say thank you. And I needed, so much, to say I'm sorry.

it was always eve's first

How did it happen?
Ribs placed like ladder steps you could cling to,
heart protection, and how still we wait for the breaking.
All those years of feeling them, the rise and fall of them,
lined palm placed against skin that bends over bone.
How I used to lay there and count them, as if one might go
missing.
How I pretended they were arrows, pointing the way.
How did I miss it all those years, that the cage of ribs might
crash into light like wings?

marriage

You wanted something broken.
I wanted to be whole.
It was a match made in need, and we made
marred marks and beauty of it.

Hazel

In my dreams, there is the smell of roses,
rose water,
and it fills my hair like a nest of moss and medicine.
There is the iris.
And there are these large rocks, and there is
quartz I claimed as diamonds.
There are the mountains.
There is the chocolate and pie crust and mulberries.
There is dish soap, and a torn apron, and hands that hold the
needle and thread and in the dream,
I slip through the eye.

trigger warning

It was all love, even though
it would be hard to understand
if you saw only the carnage.

How sometimes, the fact that you can
survive so much is, itself, the most horrible hurt.
That you are here these years later,
watering a garden plot and installing the box
fan into the window and then you are there one morning
looking into the mirror at your wet hair and your tender veins
and you do not know how to reconcile
where you came from and where you stand,
and the love feels like it will undo you.

safe passage

If you travel far enough, you find the places
where all things intersect,
how this once abandoned thread of a thing was always
winding its way toward the river.
How this moment you had imagined would be a kind of
forever, was only just the opening,
before your life expanded out in all directions.
How all beginnings begin at the end.
How we are so much, so many.

If you travel far enough, you understand wholeness,
all the things you cannot bring with you
all the things that will never leave.
And so you are standing there in the kitchen,
coffee dripping from paper filter to cup,
surrounded by presents of love for the lit dark
and this is the truth.
To say I want to travel everywhere with you, is to say
I love you, complete.
I want to know all of you. Show me the way.

legion heart

birch tree heart.
sugared hands and salted limes heart.
sailor's knot heart, twined and twisted.
horses running wild heart,
walking on my hands heart.
poison ivy heart. orange glow of the cigarette
lit in the dark heart.
gravel heart.
honeysuckle heart.
heart of spilled ink, strawberries and silk scarves.
whispering secrets in the dark heart.
brick laying heart.
metal blades and snake skin heart.
water shaking against the shore heart.
heart of soft peach skin, part sweet part bite.
heart of hip bones and clay.
gravity heart, bringing me back to solid ground.
ache in the back of my heated throat heart.

heart like a flickering neon sign, like good medicine,
like veins of aquamarine and onyx,
like a thunderstorm, crashing and then calm.
listen to me. your hunting heart, your greenhouse heart,
your heart of heat and seaweed and thunderstorms,
deer antlers and atlases. you can trust it. i promise.

(un) holy HYMNS
to the human

[him/]

noun

1. a secular psalm or poem of praise to
   the broken and the beautiful,
   belonging to the body and good earth.
2. when there are no answers,
   and only art will do.
3. hedonistic honoring. also, celebration.
4. love, for what the living do.

what matters

Not that we conquered or controlled
and called it progress,
but that we are kind.
To one another. To our own being and becoming.
To the stumbling of one life into the next,
all awkward and angular limbs,
heart beating so loud it bangs open all the doors.

tryst

I am angled intersections, not whole
but complete, carried through by stormed
strength and fullness of grace.
I am a name on the tongue I do not yet speak,
not here and then here, soft skin in heat.
I am missing what was finally found,
curse words and love words written in paint sprayed clamoring
against concrete buildings.
I am a body who had cancer, with now worn bones that can no
longer box, bear the weight of
hip socket eroding in the hard push down, or bend joint
around a pole in the sustained swing.
I am one who doesn't know then, yet, how to move.

This Monday of soft gray, thrown knives and orange peels.
This need to lay down the insistence of being
right or fear of being wrong.
This question I gave up ever answering a long time ago, and
still carry in the clenched jaw.
I am the woman who once painted secret messages on the
inside of the bathtub, and a child who climbed, and an
unfinished revolution.

Lila

Heat and machete[33] and the liquid
running over hands and into all you once thought you
could outrun.

[33] a gathering of grief

the mouths of origin myths

Sometimes I think summer exits purely for the love of
bare legs and shoulders,
ice against hot skin,
and the waking of old stories ready to be written.

Babel

I once knew my body only as the site for exchange and
transaction, function and fear,
danger and the terrible loveliness of want.

Years. Decades.
Burned and bruised and tortured to numb.
Is it any wonder then I shut it down?
So can we even call it a surprise that when I first began to
hear her,
it was like she was speaking in tongues to me?

I bought disembodied books as if they could be translators,
poured over their pages looking for the decoder ring
to tell me what a torn muscle of memory means,
and a lung that clamps closed when night comes,
and the shiver when sitting in the throb of sun.

There is no place to place the unthinkable, unspeakable,
unimaginable, the tendons grown weary when twisted tight.
None of the languages ever align.

So I just stopped,
long enough to listen,
let her say what she would say
and trust there is space enough for all the things,
my body big enough,
legion,
known and unknown.

without question

I believe you.

It really did happen. The night that is still remembered only in these broken shards, because that is how it is when stuck inside the suffocation of trauma, how the mind fixates on strange particulars and blurs out what feels like too muchness. The way it felt when you heard what happened. The morning when they were just gone. The long fight to get from there to here.

I believe you.

I trust your experience and your knowing and your ways of making meaning. I believe in your strength. I believe in your choice, you silence and your voice. I believe in your courage and the marks on your skin that say where the hurt came in. I believe in your quiet and your battle cry.

I believe you.

the open earth

Spring is bended and brutal, and I watch it outside the window,
wear the weight of it inside in bones

    all of it a kind of madness.

The breaking required
to come up through a ground that may still freeze.
The audacity of the reveal, a want willing to be unveiled.
The bare skin that soaks in sun only to burn in the ice.

Is it courage or crazy to open anyway?
Is it fragile or resilient to grow green without guarantee?
Is it reckless or wild wisdom to awaken?
And what if the answer is

    yes. Both.

like this

When the windows are still open and the late night city summer sounds mix with music that fills the room and body. When the love came, knees skinned from falling, but there is no suffering. When the words are turned to worlds and you forget your laundry in the basement, and don't even care. When timing is not a thief but comes bearing unexpected presents, carried on strong shoulders and hard won histories. When your muse returns and he is smoke and sugar sweet. And your neck still remembers the mouth and all there is to do that would make any sense at all is bake pie and trace bare feet on the floor, dance moves coming back to you the way you still speak German in your dreams. And she will soon be here.

how much

would it have been enough, to have been worth
this, the being here alive,
for honest need and the sky stormed
to restless green, skin against skin,
lilacs in late may, love touched for the wet and the bare
shoulder and the night the locusts were
louder than our coming
together,
love even for the dark box, even for the angled scar,
even for unknowable,
even, especially, for the body returned to belonging?

yes.

epoch

I love the deepening etchings of history
that imprint on my face, that curve around mouth.
I earned them, in war and intimacy and abandon.

even after all these years

The body that shows the map of injuries and knows a thirst like
hunger crowding the confines of clean and cannot bear to be
touched lightly but only strong and sure, the way you might
press down hard to try to stop the bleeding.
The haunting of hunting season and the hallowed spaces
where you dug out the decay with bruised arms and the way
sometimes still, even after all these years, you still feel the way
two o'clock tastes on the mouth, filled with broken
conquests and steam rising from the concrete,
and somewhere in the space where shoulder blades
attempt to touch in the chest opening, you still miss it.
The never being able to quite find the right language
to say what really happened.
The nightmares that never leave.
The reckless glory of a waterfall washing over you,
the sound of it like a roar, and the way she brought you coffee
in bed and the plant that hung there in the shower, spilling
down like there was still time enough for
everything that came after.
The scars that formed on the inside of skin,
intimate and devastating, invisible to the rushing world.[34]

[34] the wages of grief

immunization

Five in the arms.
The ache whose origins are even deeper.
Flush of fever and questions of memory and how
all I want is ice and blueberry pie and no translation.

When did we begin telling ourselves we were ever immune?
Life is far too intimate, a knot of ache and stillness.
So we move slow as the heat, turn heads from side to side,
wondering when something like breathing became so
beautiful.

wage peace

Return to source, the cusp of creation, the wreckage of want.
Be your own witness. The strong anchor of this,
the soft curve where mouths move.
Make things.
Ask questions.
Become a house of safekeeping, occupying space,
willing to open the window up on the third floor where
hunger could swim out to wet air and late summer sounds
could murmur and shake into a room and bed and love.
Walk by water.
Take your hair down and let it fill hands and cover shoulders.
Get in a car and drive for as long as you need and
if your grief goes into bargaining, promise
you will turn around the moment the sky blinks.
Believe yourself.
Pray to your own torn hands.
Paint the walls a green so dark its gray, no black, like
river rock, cold and smooth to the touch.
Read things.
Step inside a greenhouse and know new the meaning of your
own words. *I love you.* Mad and raging,
stung and sensitive as the skin of peaches,
unknowing and returned to reason, I love you.
And how in this moment
the love splintered into something like light.

survivor

when bitter is also beautiful.
kiss the scars that tell the stories.
with love, for the warriors.

recipe for winter

Wrestle well, bodies flipped and breathing deep.
Listen for the ocean.
Enter the scared without knowing where it will ruin you.
Tend to your dark.
Taste salt and chocolate and a pink sky for breakfast.
Change your mind, without apology.
Tell your story in any order you want, no need for the
constraints of chronology.
Tell your story as if the ending is not yet known.
Welcome the thick white of fog and the soft white of snow and
the quiet of seeing your own breath rise in the restless night.
Work for justice.
Say no with all the clarity of your body
knowing the edge of endings.
Tongue kiss yes.
Ask good questions. Wear belonging around your neck,
silver slipping under the shirt and cool against skin.
Emancipate your want.
Set a seat at the table for your own inner outcast.
Eat real food and real words. Wake your own wisdom.

the owls are not what they seem: possibility

1. There could be time still, time enough for days on a sectional couch, reading, close, time enough for what matters.

2. The answer to the question you've been afraid to ask, could be yes.

3. The water could root you, and the ground could carry you to the other side.

4. Love could not hurt, and walk with you into an unknown future, gentle and rich.

5. It could turn out that nothing is wasted.

6. You could choose only that which is effortless and meaningful.

7. You could leave the garden. You could name your own animals. You could sit there in the matchbox bar, late at night with smudged eye makeup as the cold starts to come in, and know your answer in that moment as true. *When did it happen?* she asked. *How did you know, that your life belonged to you now?* (And I didn't realize the answer until it came spilling out of my mouth. *When nothing, not a single thing, was forbidden.* Then I could take full responsibility. Then I could truly choose. Then I could love free.)

8. The writing on the wall could spell out your dirt roads of satisfaction and bodied epiphanies.

9. It could happen. You know this, right? You could lay down your swords and kiss your scars and make altars of your wrecked and insistent fate line, make a bed of rosewater and skin, make a home of hard laughter and second acts and your undoing disbelief.

the breath became flesh

The love living in the lining of my skin
is like stories,
so many stories.
How depending on the day or the way the sun
hits the angles of face and clavicle,
the story will be distinct, different, a tongue that tells
secrets and one that speaks simple.

Is like roads on a map of the palm,
read for clues and compass.
Is like being breathed back to life when you thought the
fire had consumed even the fight.
Is like shadow pictures on the wall made with deft hands,
drowsy with memories of
who we were going to grow up to become.
Is like reading water, is like drinking home.

Living in the lining of my skin is a language,
and when all the words disappear,
here is where she speaks to me.

mutual regard

"He really liked birds, didn't he?"[35] he says.
"That was your first word. Did you know that?" I say.
"What?"
"Bird. Your first word was bird. And you'd stand at the window
and jab your baby hands at the glass,
pointing at them, saying the word, again and again."
"It wasn't mom? Or mama?"
"No. It was bird. You wanted them to stay. But they were
always leaving. And I used to be so afraid of them, of birds,
before you were born."
"Why?"
"Because they always felt like they were about ready to lose
something. The way their heads look scared, waiting.
And I wanted to leave too, except I couldn't fly away."
"But not anymore," he says
"No. Not anymore," I say.
"You just stopped being afraid?"
"I think I just loved you more.

[35] Jean Luc Mylayne, *No. 524*

first things

Flowers on a fire escape. Walking out in the mornings, hand warmed around coffee swirled with cream. The kind of mornings when heat rises off sidewalk and street and what you long for lingers just beneath skin, and with the sound of the train rumbling and the feel of fern leaves, you remember how to listen to what you knew before you were filled with everyone else's ideas.

there will your treasure be

Bone scans and bitter cold. Packed boxes and unkempt words. Lumber at the hardware store and cocktails at the hotel with mirrors for walls that glitter in ricocheted light. Relics and ruins, inked beginnings and true choice. Knowing how much I do not know (and willing to learn even as it injures, because the discomfort is a kindness). Cold raspberries and stained lips kissing.

Life, like my heart, is messy and complete.

center of the x

Trusting my yes and my no,
my hearts half dark half feather winged knowing.
This is my one life, and I'm trusting myself.

full of grace

The baths. Long waits, and people singing as everyone stands and sits in unending lines. And then it is your turn. And the robed women are asking you what language you speak, and saying to find your intention. And you are standing in front of the curtain and everyone stops. You wonder if you remember any prayer in any language. You wonder what it means. And then you cross over and the white sheet is so cold, and hugged around you, and they hold your hands while you hear your own hedonistic heart, and plunge, and reach out to the statue of her, Mary. And the water. It is so, so cold. And then you leave, dressed again, and it is true, what they had said, about how the water dries instantly. And you cannot stop crying and everyone around you nods quietly, smiling.[36]

---

[36] piscines

we were just waiting for our fate to open

Grit and glitter, open palms and unknown outcomes,
salt on the skin and Nina Simone singing slow,
slipping into the space between heart and mouth.[37]

[37] the night before everything changed.

do you want this or that? he asked.
my answer: *yes*.

The feelings don't have to add up or make sense or create a tidy portrait of the life you thought you would have. You get to miss her terribly and still feel the relief of having space again to move easy. You can burn with anger and choose to spend an entire day riding the train to nowhere and want to let it go and not let it go. You can relentlessly hurt from the loss of him and be stunned by the flutter of fascination when you said yes, and you can feel conflicted and guilty and grief and sultry joy. You get to make a big deal of your success and hide out in the bath and feel forever stuck in strange time travel. You are allowed your howl, your silence, your throat burning with things left unspoken and your hands pumping on your own heart.

Your smile when you catch your reflection in the window glass while walking, and your misunderstandings, and your swallowed revenge. Your bar fight and your slow dance and your unfinished words. Your contentment and your hunger and your sting of knowing they all moved on. Your eagerness to make things right and your need to lose time and your collection of rockets you will one day send into a blank and waiting sky.

There is a lie we are fed that says feelings have to line up like links in a chain and that inside the fence is all the space we are allowed. But your open emotions and experiences, your life, belongs to you, and you get to own all of it. The life you thought you would have, was an idea. And you are flesh and feeling, blood and bone, breath and mess of beautiful maddening contradictions, complete.

assumption of mystery

To bloom must be the most violent and gorgeous act possible,
defiant and close, unwilling to wait
because this is your real life, and so
why not show your hand and your colors, trust that an
unclenched fist will spill honeycomb and new language.

I would like, I think, to bloom like this.
Like the sounds of locusts and trees speaking.
Like the sound of the earth breathing.

epiphany

This morning. Bill Withers playing loudly, coffee cooling in the cup on the bathroom sink where I'm standing there, comb and hairspray in hand, helping him with his hair. Because it's unruly coarse and stands up straight in thick shocks of red. It bothers him. So he has in this rare moment asked for help. So I am. I am standing there helping him, teaching him how to wrangle the thickness and we're singing under our breath and he is smiling at himself in the mirror and I have that crashing into my reflection moment, when I look up and realize I am a mother. I am his mother, for here and forever. And I think to myself, I would like to remember this beautifully uneventful and human morning for the rest of my life.

I would be satisfied

I want to fill trees with lights and spider's silk
intricate as lace.
I want to fill a canyon with the echoed sound of
wild horses running through ocean.
I want to fill my bathtub with magnolias.
I want to fill my fists with the color of cherry blossoms and
secular hymns.[38]

[38] I claim them all:

to my eighteen-year old self

Some things it is worthwhile to learn and know how to do.

How to check the oil in your car, how to buy a car,
how to drive across the country alone and in love,
how to navigate public transportation.
When to leave a business partnership, a lover, a party.
How to mix a cocktail and make soufflé and hula hoop.
How to use a power drill and paint your own apartment and
love what is aching and beautifully real.
The way you like to be touched. Your own creative cadence.
The reason for your rebellion.
How to give a toast, and tell a story,
and stand full and still in your power.

Kiki de Montparnasse

After more blood slips from skin to needle to waiting vial, and
the bones wait for scans and answers.
After minding gaps and broken boots in the storm; after lists of
things that will happen or not happen.

You think, *I am so hungry*. All of me.

So you leave the unfinished things and ride the subway
through snow and weathered people.
You walk into and through art, stopped silent in the staring,
fed to full.
Exhibits about movement in art and architecture, but
it's not just about what happened when cities
fractured through pastoral painting. It is about you. About us.
How we take what is broken and make things.
And then you turn a corner and it is there, tree trunk rings
rippled over flesh, scratched film playing on a loop,
as if hypnotized, mesmerized.
Return to Reason. And you know now what this means.

come to light

full like the word lust rounds in the mouth.
low and heavy, intimate and unapologetic.
the glow of it. the wonder.
the gold to pink to red.[39]
dear god she's beautiful.

---

[39] the magic moon

talking back

What if there is nothing wrong with you, with what you want,
with your legs and your ambition,
your softness and your redwood solid strength?

What then?

unholy pilgrimage

(you are allowed)

Which is to say our tension between the languages we live within and never fully translate; which is to say the contradictions we can neither explain nor understand in full and so maybe we could just show up and love them. Love the mess of parts and pieces that clash and collide and cohabitate, the raw and open edged elements from which creation herself comes. There is no failure in falling in love with our humanity, showing up in our inconsistencies, forever finding truth in what happens in all the spaces in-between. There is no wrong in changing one's mind, in knowing and not knowing, in wanting what does not belong and yet still inside of us the parts keep knotting themselves around one another, demanding our attention and asking the exiled in us to be invited in. We are, all of us, so much, so many. Devoted and dirty, the rush of doing and the hours staring at the wall, and is this losing or finding or both. The articulation lit up with emerging imagination, the years you gave to penance and the years you turned away and crashed into light. The heathen and holy, deferring and defiant. The moment you wanted to never come back. The moment you would have done anything to make them stay. The terrible heave of grief and the tremor disrupting your ideals when the ecstatic slipped in like a cat in the near night, right before sunrise. Your piles of books and your mountains as medicine. You are allowed your fluid and your firm grip, your bite and your kiss. They don't have to add up to whole that matches or makes sense, where everything fits inside itself. This being human thing is messy, and it is a power, and it is a love, as beautiful to me as the blue neon that hums in my room, flickering out onto walls and words I once told myself could never be mine.

remembering forward

I remember sitting there once, legs flung akimbo, while we both stared out toward the line where ocean disappears into sky. I remember sitting there and her turning to me, thick in the middle of our corridor expanse conversation, and everything was altered. I remember the moment when nothing was forbidden, and freedom meant having all of me, without requiring constant explanation of justification. I remember how I woke that one morning in the heavy air of July, and for reasons I will never be able to understand, something in me cracked so far open that the slightest whisper of breeze against skin would have felt like electricity alive in the veins, and so I stayed there, quiet in the awakening, falling in love with the sublime taste of knowing my body as the house where I would worship.

I remember how her mouth was like origami, a paper crane I'd try to unravel and swim upon into the sea brine and how even though I have no belief in a god the way she did, my prayer was just as real. I remember how laughter was like medicine and as important to sex as mouths and skin, and what a relief it was, to come so stunningly undone. I remember the white sheets, and the voicing of want, and the being met right inside the place where words will no longer work. I remember all the times when I knew my own desire, and took the risks to speak into a world as one who was welcomed,[40] and walk into the unknown.

[40] the erotic and the holy

belonging

I know who my body will return to, even after I am gone.
I know my person and place of belonging.
Her,[41] woman, the one who I know and feel as
deeply as I do my own cells.
How do we get so lucky, after all this time and all this loss,
to find and be found?
I do not know the answer, only that I know now who my body
will return to.
Cold metal against warm skin. Love, and life before death.

---

41 beloved

I choose you

not always, but sometimes, the body heals itself. the one you always were searching for is finally found. the ambivalence requires no resolution. the fog comes thick around as you drive by a lake with the roofs opened and it occurs to you that the word mercy might mean something after all, be the hinge that the door rests open upon. you give your life to know your freedom. the hungry ghost of restless ambition leaves late in the night, slipped out unnoticed, and you wake to realize you know now reunion and something is complete. not always, but

sometimes. today.

three things

A piece of glass that fell off the disco ball.
A post it note that delivered me.
A key that opens a lock only I know.[42]

[42] treasures

fly away home

When the dish fell from your hand
shattering all over the kitchen floor,
you went to cry, from frustration and anger and fatigue,
one more thing messed up.
Just before the tears came you realized you had never, ever
liked those dishes anyway.
Do you remember this
how you then stood there, that afternoon, and
broke them all, one by one?
And how, soon after, everything changed.

recovery

"I don't understand," I said.
"What part?" he said.
"Anything," I said.

(and I think, what I really meant here was everything.)

"So maybe we don't have to understand any of it. Or maybe there is nothing to understand."
And just like that, I was free.

how much a heart can hold

The newborn baby held and the room where I sit with lovers knowing the honest abandon in naming safe words. The sea knots in bed heavy hair. The thinking through smashed structures where the words could roam free. Sanctuary, below what is beneath, lush and ripped. What do you name that kind of honor, to walk into the room where all the real things live? The grapes, purple so dark its black. The glitter that fell from someone's hand while we all walked by on concrete streets and heavy white of sky. The words that shake like lightning. Breath - taken, given. The man who called everyone he spoke to, Madame. The philosophy that illuminates but will never save you. The relief to let go the seeking of all salvation, and the bite marks made in the bicep, and the spiritual story you are writing that speaks of terror and a fist and the night you sat on the steps after midnight when the whole city woke in the heat wave. The fishnets I wear while working, sitting here, following the map splayed and tacked and taped to the wall, writing this and this and then this; the smallest black diamonds intersecting against soft skin, the tear that runs up the right thigh. Life. This day. My deepest devotion. You, strange and magnificent, messy and wide as water, a dirt smeared and sparkling mystery to me.

Caroline

When the sun starts to go gold against brick and building
and the el heaves itself over clanking track,
I think, *this is enough*.
How in these seconds here and then passed,
when I looked up and saw what was real and the day was
smashing into night, nothing else mattered.
I always want more, to devour the world with wonder and
depth and the bite of particularity and inimitable embraces.
But is it not also true, that in those moments,[43]
this aching arched light, it is itself the whole world?

[43] They are, I swear, enough, reasons to live

strong medicine

There were hot springs in New Mexico, and we took off all our
clothes and submerged skin inside and underneath the
warm, with six women beside me,
steam rising from the top of the water and you could
breathe it in, like smoke rising.
Here, where they held me up and I was surrounded.

It was only two weeks after cancer.

And there are many things that may not cure,
but there can be no question that they heal.

the demon you can swallow gives you it's power

When you know you are both broken and met.
When that which will haunt you forever and that which
you most love, collide
and so the door opens and the neon in the night
spills out blue[44] like grief could belong with the
richest lust and most intimate love,
like even an alley cat might find her way home.
The door opens and signs glow true and so I'm standing there,
crashing and collapsing and quiet and undone,
wiping the salt and wet from my face.
She was there. And then the rain came.
Amor fati, the love of your fate, which is your life.

---

[44] the most beautiful gift I have ever received

born from the storm

From the moment I was thrust in to you,
we've been wrestling our way into freedom and intimacy.

rush in

With the feel of cotton and silk against skin upon first waking.
With the sun when it cracks through window blinds,
rises up from earth.
With the masses and the precise particular, the people,
all the people crowded with desire and the most private hurts
and the way we shimmer without even knowing
and the way we sometimes look up from our own distractions
and make eye contact and in those moments see what was for
no reason and every reason, waiting to undo us into a thick
mess of what we once imaged we would escape.
With the shape of her curved and angled back.
With the corporeal and the taste of salt and the way the
feelings roar like waves in the body.
With the relief when the fist unclenches
and with the way words feel in the mouth.
And with you.[45]

---

[45] the falling in love with you.

the calling

Because the dreams of the quarries returned (the unknown of what rests beneath, welcome and wanted, right after crashing into cold water, how it would almost feel like flying more than falling on the way down). And so too did the late summer plums.

Because a man once walked an unauthorized high wire between the Twin Towers in New York city on an August morning to discard . . . and reinvent his art.

Because the ankle strap on my orange vintage shoe broke that night, and when I asked if she had a safety pin, she said, "Here, what size do you wear? You can wear mine."

Olly-olly oxen free. Because in the end, Eros was burned by the light, and this was his strange salvation.

Because when I was seventeen, I sat in high school English class and wrote out the poems we studied onto my skin, pale flesh of thigh and arm up to elbow, with a ballpoint pen. This is what I know of trust.

Because there was a plant cutting, in a glass jar, sitting there in the shower among soap and it was beautiful, a thing so hopeful and regenerative. And how else do you explain it except say this was the moment when I knew.

Because when Jacob wrestled with the angel, the wounding was the blessing. And the ladder goes in both directions.

Because when I stood outside in the night, looking up at the Moon with him, this boy that came from my body and is forever his own, I knew he was the purest and most complicated love I will ever know.

Because some people speak of a calling as clouds clearing, a great voice from the other side of the woods, and a path opened like seas parted or cornfields after the crop has been harvested and now you can see again to the place where ground meets sky. And I do not have or know this. Or if it happens, I have yet to recognize my own name. Still, I'm walking in.

Because in the dream, she told me the name of trees and I wondered if they were scarred or marked as chosen, when names were carved into wood, and if they knew or cared or made such a distinction, or if this was only mine.

Because in those stories, she opens and she eats and she sees.

Because, when we had coffee that last time, before he moved back to Iran, he told me, "You are perhaps mistaken. You are not a rebel, going against the rules given you. You may be outlaw here. But it's more. It is so much more. You are simply your own country."

Because she survived her past to arrive in the present. And you can call it whatever you want: the wounds of adaptation, luck, relentless hard work. Whatever name given, I will take back the year that the locusts have eaten, sit out on the back steps in the last cling of heat, her mouth like honey and wine.

Because my love is for reality, what is here, and only ever here, once.

Because of all of this, these things, I want to say that yes, maybe it is true, I have what I once assumed foreign or unfit for my temperament and terrible stories. A kind of fidelity or conviction in the movement towards light, even as we walk on the dark ground we will return to. A stillness in the unanswerable questions. A choice to create a geography of meaning. (*faith*)

footnotes: between the in-between

[1] (this was one of those)
[2] the question asked when helping a friend of eleven years move out of her house and into her life, five years after she had done the same for me.
[3] walking on the tops of tall buildings,
[4] naming
[5] what changes in a year:
[6] birth,
[7] liminal space,
[8] the unlocking with my own keyed arm and hand,
[9] for integration is not merger.

[10] Susan speaks
[11] answers to the questions that live beyond language.
[12] Tell the most real story:
[13] Lourdes,
[14] consent,
[15] You, Mexico.

[16] What does it feel like, she asked me.
This, I said.
What, she said.
Fire, I said. I'm on fire.

[17 (] My son at eleven.
[18] The year my life belonged to me.)

19 *Listen*.
Ok, I said.
I'm listening,
20 to the good body, my body.
21 this is a map of the flesh,
22 story of scars
23 to a full moon.

24 Communion:
25 the year I had cancer for the second time,
26 two years after the wall fell,
27 the importance of words
28 [in] beauty standards.

29 [for there is] refuge in words.
30 Naming my own animals,
31 this was my liberation.

32 After the brutality of illness,
33 a gathering of grief
34 the wages of grief
35 [like] Jean Luc Mylayne, N*o. 524*
36 [like] piscines
37 [like] the night before everything changed.

38 I claim them all:
39 the magic moon,
40 the erotic and the holy
41 beloved 42 treasures.

43 They are, I swear, enough, reasons to live
44 the most beautiful gift I have ever received
45 the falling in love with you.

greenhouse love

Lying upside down,
flung over the bed with legs wrapped around longing,
while piles of unkempt things topple over beside me.

There is the fan and the humidity climbing ivy and the
soft white like flowers,
and my questions taste like salt and honey.

I am wondering what the past knows; my own
memories forged on mountains, and a belief in the
freedom and sequins of Rockettes, and a slashed scar that runs
down my back.

Hands opened out toward the Blue Moon lit love of a life I now
know as belonging to me,
bodies at rest beside one another and
her face waiting
for me,
the tangerine and almost chilled cream we will eat late
tonight with fingers and spoons.

After all these years, alone, to now know
the finding and found.
How impossible
how real
how we choose life, again and again and again.

once in a blue moon

The past will return to you, or you to it and you will know then
what can never be undone and what can be burned to release.
You will learn the legacy of your own heart still beating.
The night will warm.
The woman will stay.
The spider web will spin silk, net itself over stairs and
between the beams of wood that break the fall.
You will survive the loss, and walk
wounded and want, still, to live forever.
You will drink warm liquor, and eat ice cubes, and your stories will
meet the horizon of your body made of bone and red and water.
You will spend your days and nights worried and wondering
and then no more.
You will swim in an abandoned cenote and breathe underwater.
You will dance hip sways of honey. You will remember.
You will forget. You will close the vault door.
You will open all the cages and watch birds fly away home.
You will wake in the night to the word rapture.
The magician will stick his hand in the hat and instead of the
rabbit or fabric flowers or flutter of doves, it will be birch trees and
paths uncrossed and days filled with nothing but white sky.
Your mouth will fill with persimmon, and your arms will fill
with the unrelenting want of her, and your light will make way
for unknown answers, ricocheting out and onto everything.
Once in a blue moon, you will say the words I love you, and
they will be made new.

Acknowledgments

My gratitude

To the world which spit me out, and the world which welcomed me whole

To the storm chaser, and to the stretched wide road, and to the night when I left so I could finally find home

To my son, who for months ate takeout for dinner and who rescued my lost words and who let me be his mother

To my maternal grandmother Judy, who taught me to love beauty

To the professor at University all those years ago, who told me I could write and told me to keep writing, who gave me permission to cut out the tongues of others in my language, and tell my own story instead

To the lake cottage, the blue chair, the boat house where I write, the sounds of water, the coffee in the morning, and the forever friend who gives me the key and her love

To Bryonie Wise, who edited and cared for my words with elegance and devotion

To Stacy De La Rosa, my partner in art, whose ribcage and heart complete creation

To kvv my love, who showed me what it is to believe

To those who speak the word, and have fallen in love with the words we made flesh, breath after breath

To the ocean and jungle and city streets of Mexico, and the back steps of the fire escape where I began those years ago

Thank you, thank you, thank you

Isabel Abbott.
writer. activist. corporeal artist.
sanctuary in birth, sex, and death.
love for the holy and hedonistic hearts.
www.isabelabbott.com

Made in the USA
San Bernardino, CA
28 December 2019